Why Study 1, 2, and 3 John?

I can think of two seasons in my l   elt very little assurance that I was a   ss, or his faithfulness to his promise   ;. I was seeking to follow God's way   n't feel like I had really come to know ımm.

When I have been in that state, needing assurance, it is to the writings of John that I have turned—especially his first, much longer letter.

You will already know John as one of the Gospel writers—but his purpose in writing these letters is different from his purpose in writing his account of Jesus' life. In John's Gospel, he wrote so "that you may believe that Jesus is the Messiah, the Son of God, and that by believing you may have life in his name" (John 20:31). The Gospel was written to help people believe. But John's first letter was written to help believers *know* that they believe.

John, led by the Holy Spirit, assumes there will be followers of Jesus who struggle to know if they truly have come to know him. It is a comfort to know that such struggles are not unexpected! God is not frustrated with us for experiencing such need. Indeed, his heart is to help us.

In his first letter, John's concern is to reassure his readers that they are in the truth and that they have eternal life—while making it clear that the false teachers who were infecting the church were not and did not! John sets out three tests which he revisits throughout the letter, concerning doctrine, love, and obedience. These tests are given to provide assurance, helping us to see the ways we sincerely do believe Jesus, seek to follow his commands, and love his people—albeit imperfectly.

John's second and third letters are much shorter. You will spot the same themes of doctrine, love, and obedience. But these letters are written to more specific audiences and contain more practical and detailed instructions about how to walk in the truth of the gospel.

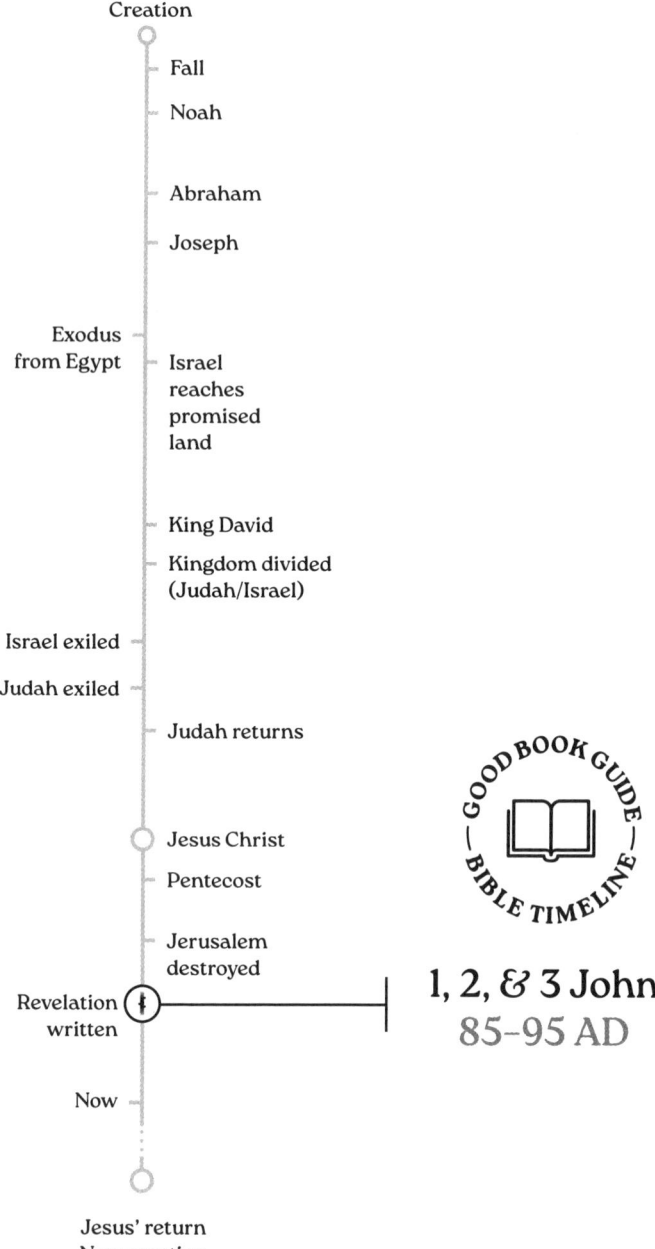

Creation

Fall

Noah

Abraham

Joseph

Exodus
from Egypt

Israel
reaches
promised
land

King David

Kingdom divided
(Judah/Israel)

Israel exiled

Judah exiled

Judah returns

GOOD BOOK GUIDE
BIBLE TIMELINE

Jesus Christ

Pentecost

Jerusalem
destroyed

Revelation
written

1, 2, & 3 John
85-95 AD

Now

Jesus' return
New creation

Sam Allberry

1, 2, & 3 John

Joyful Certainty

◔ **7-Session Bible Study**

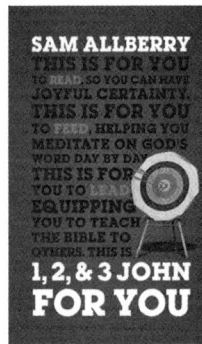

1, 2, & 3 John For You

These studies are adapted from *1, 2, & 3 John For You*. If you are reading *1, 2, & 3 John For You* alongside this Good Book Guide, here is how the studies in this booklet link to the chapters of *1, 2, & 3 John For You*:

Study 1 > Ch 1-2
Study 2 > Ch 3
Study 3 > Ch 4
Study 4 > Ch 5-6

Study 5 > Ch 7
Study 6 > Ch 8
Study 7 > Ch 9

Find out more about *1, 2, & 3 John For You* at: www.thegoodbook.com/for-you

1, 2, & 3 John: Joyful Certainty
A Good Book Guide
© Sam Allberry/The Good Book Company, 2025.

Published by The Good Book Company

thegoodbook.com | thegoodbook.co.uk
thegoodbook.com.au | thegoodbook.co.nz

A CIP catalogue record for this book is available from the British Library.

Published in association with the literary agency of Wolgemuth & Wilson.

Design by André Parker and Drew McCall

ISBN: 9781802543049 | JOB-008070 | Printed in Turkey

Contents

Introduction

One of the Bible writers described God's word as "a lamp for my feet, a light on my path" (Psalm 119:105, NIV). God gave us the Bible to tell us about who he is and what he wants for us. He speaks through it by his Spirit and lights our way through life.

That means that we need to look carefully at the Bible and uncover its meaning—but we also need to apply what we've discovered to our lives.

Good Book Guides are designed to help you do just that. The sessions in this book are interactive and easy to lead. They're perfect for use in groups or for personal study.

Let's take a look at what is included in each session.

Talkabout: Every session starts with an ice-breaker question, designed to get people talking around a subject that links to the Bible study.

Investigate: These questions help you explore what the passage is about.

Apply: These questions are designed to get you thinking practically: what does this Bible teaching mean for you and your church?

Explore More: These optional sections help you to go deeper or to explore another part of the Bible which connects with the main passage.

Getting Personal: These sections are a chance for personal reflection. Some groups may feel comfortable discussing these, but you may prefer to look at them quietly as individuals instead—or leave them out.

Pray: Here, you're invited to pray in the light of the truths and challenges you've seen in the study.

Each session is also designed to be easily split into two! Watch out for the **Apply** section that comes halfway through, and stop there if you haven't got time to do the whole thing in one go.

In the back of the book, you'll find a **Leader's Guide**, which provides helpful notes on every question, along with everything else that group leaders need in order to facilitate a great session and help the group uncover the riches of God's light-giving word.

1

The Real Jesus

1 John 1:1 - 2:2

Talkabout

1. How do people in today's world try to find out about God, or about the meaning of life?

Investigate

📖 **Read 1 John 1:1-4**

DICTIONARY

Testify (v 2): talk about something as a witness, as if in court.

John is talking about Jesus in these verses. He calls him "the Word of life."

2. How does John emphasize the fact that he really knows about Jesus? What words does he use?

3. But it's clear that Jesus isn't like every other person you might see and touch. How does John highlight this? Pick out the key phrases.

Explore More | OPTIONAL

Jesus himself made the same claims that John is making about him.

📖 Read John 8:48-59

Jesus claimed to have existed before Abraham, and he referred to himself as "I am"—the name God gave himself at the time of the Exodus (v 58).

- Why was this so controversial to his opponents?
- What else did Jesus say that shows us who he is?
- How did Abraham respond to the thought of Jesus' coming?

---

4. In verses 3 and 4, what is the result of Jesus having appeared and John having seen him and talked about him?

Apply

5. How could this passage reassure someone who…
   - is worried that they are not a very good Christian because they don't know enough?

   - feels sad that they missed out on seeing Jesus in the flesh?

- is doubtful about whether God exists at all?

Getting Personal | OPTIONAL

We can be in a living relationship with Jesus today through receiving with faith the message John is sharing. We have true fellowship with the Father and with Jesus Christ (v 3)!

What is your relationship with Jesus like? Can you find assurance in this passage for when you feel distant from him?

Investigate

📖 **Read 1 John 1:5 – 2:2**

Jesus really did come. But why does this matter so much? It matters that Jesus is real because we have a real problem that we need him to solve: our sin.

6. John mentions three claims people might make (1:6, 8, 10). Look at the first claim. Given that John has just said that God is light, what do you think it means to walk in the darkness?

- What might it look like for someone to claim that they have fellowship with God while walking in the darkness?

7. Look at the claims in verses 8 and 10. What might it look like for someone to make one of these claims, and why are they wrong to do so?

8. Instead of making these claims, we should acknowledge and confess our sin. Why do you think this can sometimes be so hard to do?

- But what is our great hope and motivation (v 7, 9)?

Getting Personal | OPTIONAL

Can you identify any of the "claims" in your own attitudes? Are there areas of your life where you need to let God's light expose your darkness?

It may be painful to confess your sin, but it is always worth it.

---

9. What is John's hope for his readers (2:1)? How can we square this with what he has just said?

10. Look at verses 1-2. When we do sin, why is it significant that Jesus is…
   • our "advocate"?

   • "the Righteous One"?

   • "the atoning sacrifice"?

Apply

11. When we do sin, what should we do next? How does the identity of Jesus help us in this?

12. John wrote all of this "to make our joy complete" (1:4). What makes you feel most joyful or excited in this first part of 1 John?

Pray

Use your answers to question 12 to help you praise God. Ask him to keep on giving you the same joy in him throughout your week.

Then spend some time praying about your sin. You may like to confess your sins to one another. Whether you do that or not, cry out to the Lord together, asking him to help you to hate the sin in your lives and thanking him for sending a real Savior to deal with our real sin.

2

This Is How We Know (I)

1 John 2:3-11, 15-17

The Story So Far...

John opened his first letter joyfully, affirming that Jesus is real and we can know the truth about him—and therefore have fellowship with God despite our sin.

Talkabout

1. What might make someone doubt that their faith is really real?

Investigate

John wants to assure us that our faith is real. He is inviting us to spot the evidence of spiritual health in our own lives.

📖 **Read 1 John 2:3-6**

2. These verses give us the first way we can be sure that we know God. What is it?

3. Why might these words seem intimidating?

None of us can say we keep God's commands perfectly. But obedience doesn't have to be perfect to be real. What sets Christians apart is not that we don't sin; it's that we don't *want* to sin! We are not like Jesus yet, but we are becoming like him.

4. Can you think of a time when you've been encouraged by seeing a fellow believer seeking to obey God or seeking to battle sin?

- Can you think of a time when you've seen someone who claims to follow Jesus but doesn't seem interested in keeping his commands?

Getting Personal | OPTIONAL

Where do you see the fruit of obedience in your own life? Are there ways in which you have changed to become like Jesus as you've got to know him?

📖 Read 1 John 2:7-8

John is about to talk to us about Jesus' command to love (as we'll see in the next verses).

5. Why might it be reassuring to know that what John is about to talk about is an "old command" (v 7)?

6. But John also says it is a new command, because "its truth is seen in him" (Jesus) and "the true light is already shining" (v 8). What does this mean?

- Why is this reassuring to us as we seek to obey?

Explore More | OPTIONAL

This "old command" is what Jesus cited as the most important commandment—you might call it his executive summary of the entirety of Old Testament law.

📖 **Read Mark 12:28-31**

- Who are we to love and how much?

Apply

7. What could it look like for us to love what Jesus loved and live as he lived, even if we don't do this perfectly?

Investigate

📖 **Read 1 John 2:9-11**

Love is the second "test" by which we can know our faith is real.

8. How do we behave differently when we can see in comparison to when we're in the dark?

- What about spiritual light and darkness—how do we tell whether someone is in one or the other, according to verses 9-11?

9. The idea that our love proves whether our faith is genuine might be scary to start with—we might not feel we're loving enough. But how does this light/darkness imagery, with its very clear distinctions, help reassure us?

📖 Read 1 John 2:15-17

John now wants to show us that we can't turn *toward* God's ways without turning *away* from those that are contrary.

10. When John says "the world," what does he mean? Look at what he says in verse 16 to help you understand this.

11. What do you think it means that "the world and its desires pass away"? What evidence of this do you see in the world around you?

Getting Personal | OPTIONAL

When do you find it most tempting to "love the world"? Take time to ask God to help you to put the full weight of your life down on Jesus, loving his ways and obeying his commands.

Apply

12. John writes to reassure his readers as well as to challenge them. So, who do you know who shows evidence of true faith, and what is that evidence? How could you encourage those people this week?

- What about those you know who may be feeling doubtful or discouraged? How could you encourage them from this passage?

- What would you say to someone who is dismissing or minimizing their own sin, or treating another believer badly?

Pray

Use your answers to question 12 to pray for your Christian brothers and sisters. Ask God to grow you in obedience to him and love for one another.

3

This Is How We Know (II)

1 John 2:12-14, 18-27

Father God, you are in this room with us. You know everyone in this group. Please guide our conversations and reveal new things about yourself to us. Amen.

The Story So Far...

John opened his first letter joyfully, affirming that Jesus is real and we can know the truth about him—and therefore have fellowship with God despite our sin.

He explored two of three "tests" by which we can have assurance that our faith is genuine: obedience and love.

Talkabout

1. What would you say makes someone a real Christian? How do you know they are really saved?

19

Investigate

DICTIONARY

Antichrist (v 18): this word literally just means someone who is against Christ. Sometimes it refers to a specific opponent who is to come, but here it means anyone who opposes Jesus.

Anointing (v 20): literally this means having oil poured or rubbed on your head. It was done to priests and kings in the Old Testament, marking them as special. Now believers in Christ receive the anointing of the Holy Spirit.

John is introducing us to his third "test" by which we can know that our faith is real.

2. How can we be sure that we know God and have eternal life (v 23-25)?

3. Why does what we believe about Jesus impact whether or not we truly know God?

4. What does John say about "antichrists" (people who are opposed to Jesus)? How do we know that their faith is not genuine (v 19, 22)?

Explore More | OPTIONAL

Throughout the centuries a clock has been ticking in heaven; a timetable has been discreetly advancing. It has now reached its final stage. As John puts it, "This is the last hour" (v 18). It's crunch time.

But what is "the last hour"? It means the time between the first and second comings of Jesus.

📖 **Read Mark 13:32-37**

- What does Jesus say about his return?
- What impact should it have on us to know that it is "the last hour"?

Apply

5. Based on this passage, what might you say to someone who says they respect Jesus but just don't believe he is God?

Getting Personal | OPTIONAL

Set this book aside for a moment and ask yourself what the true posture of your heart is toward Jesus.

He is not worthy of mere reverence and respect. He is fully deserving of our full *worship* as the Son of the Father. We cannot properly honor him with anything less than this!

6. John has shown us what makes a true Christian. How might this challenge us about the way we treat other Christians who have different opinions from us?

• What about people who seem to be Christians but, according to John's definition, are not—how do you think we should treat them?

Investigate

📖 **Read 1 John 2:26-27**

DICTIONARY

Counterfeit (v 27): fake.

7. What keeps us anchored to the truth (v 26-27, and look back at verse 20)?

8. Why is this reassuring for those who fear that their faith is weak or vulnerable?

📖 **Read 1 John 2:12-14**

We've left these verses out until now because they wonderfully sum up John's message of reassurance.

9. What does John want his readers to know?

"Dear children" presumably refers to all of John's readers. "Fathers" probably means older believers (men and women) and "young men" newer ones (again, both men and women).

10. Why do you think John chose to direct specific encouragements to specific groups? Why did they need to hear these truths?

11. What do you find most encouraging in these verses?

The battle is already won. we dont [I dont need to do anything else. The answer is away from ourselves.

Apply

12. Are you ever tempted to think that your faith needs upgrading in some way—perhaps that you need special knowledge or experiences?

- How will what we've read in this study help to reassure us, and help us to remain steadfast in the faith we have received?

Getting Personal | OPTIONAL

"Just as [your anointing] has taught you, remain in him" (v 27). How will you personally put this into practice this week?

Pray

Praise God for the encouragements of this passage.

If you have not already done so, ask God to send you the Holy Spirit and teach you the truth.

Pray specifically for those who have a teaching ministry in your church. Ask God to keep them in the truth.

O Lord Jesus Christ
who art as a shadow of a great
rock in a weary land
who beholdest my weak creature
weary of labour, weary of pleasure
weary of hope deferred
weary of self
In thine abundant compassion
And fellow feeling with us
and unutterable tenderness
bring us we pray thee
unto thy rest.

4

Continue in Jesus

1 John 2:28 - 4:6

The Story So Far...

John opened his first letter joyfully, affirming that Jesus is real and we can know the truth about him—and therefore have fellowship with God despite our sin.

He explored three "tests" by which we can have assurance that our faith is genuine—obedience, love, and belief in Jesus—and urged us to remain in Christ.

Talkabout

1. What traits do people in your family have in common? Do you take after older family members? Do younger family members take after you?

Investigate

📖 **Read 1 John 2:28 – 3:10**

2. John wants us to have confidence when Jesus returns (2:28). What will give us this confidence about who we are in him (v 29)?

3. 3:1-2 is full of excitement—so what is John excited about?

• What implications do these truths have for how we live now (v 2-3)?

John has shown us how the second coming of Jesus motivates us to be holy in the present. Next he shows how the *first* coming of Jesus has given us that same motivation to live righteously and avoid sin.

4. In verses 4-10, what does John say about...
• what sin is like and where it comes from (v 4, 8)?

• what Jesus has done to our sin (v 5, 8)?

• Why is sin therefore out of place in our lives as Christians?

In verses 6 and 9-10, it sounds like John is saying that anyone who sins can't be a Christian. But he can't be saying that—look back at 1:8, where he says that if we claim to be without sin, we deceive ourselves!

John is not saying that sin is impossible for a Christian, nor that a single sin invalidates our claim to be God's children. He's talking about the trajectory of our lives. If we embrace our own sin, then we have no basis for assurance. If we oppose it, then we can know we are children of God.

Apply

5. Speaking practically, what can we actually do to oppose sin in our lives?

- According to this passage, if we are believers, what is empowering us to oppose sin and do what is right?

Getting Personal | OPTIONAL

Take time to consider if there are any ways in which you have normalized sin in your life—accepting it instead of opposing it. Who could you talk to about this? What help do you need to put that sin to death?

Take time also to reflect on the ways in which you are doing what is right and living God's way. Praise God for his work in you and for making you his child!

Investigate

📖 **Read 1 John 3:11-24**

> **DICTIONARY**
>
> **Cain** (v 12): the older son of Adam and Eve—see Genesis 4.
>
> **Condemn** (v 20): say that someone is guilty.

6. According to verses 11-18, what quality will be displayed by those who are in Christ?

- John gives us a bold definition of love in verse 16. How do you think this compares with how people in the world around us understand it?

We need this clear definition—since it's all too easy to seem righteous while not actually living a life of love.

7. How and why did Cain show the opposite of love (v 12)?

- How does John turn this example into a challenge for us (v 14-15)?

8. What's another way in which we can fail to show real love (v 17-18)?

Getting Personal | OPTIONAL

How are you doing at showing love to those around you? Take stock—or take a moment to ask a trusted friend to help you to see ways in which you are showing love and areas or relationships where you are doing less well.

---

9. Our hearts may be feeling guilty as we read these words—so what does John say to reassure us, and why is it reassuring?
- v 19-20

- v 21-22

- v 23-24

We have essentially been recapping two of John's tests: obedience (2:28 – 3:10) and love (3:11-24). Next John returns to the third test: belief.

📖 Read 1 John 4:1-6

10. What are the two crucial beliefs that John identifies (v 2-3)?

- If someone denies these truths, what does this mean?

11. There are many opinions and voices in the world that are opposed to Jesus. That might seem scary. But how does verse 4 reassure us?

Explore More | OPTIONAL

We have a lot to be excited about—but being God's children also involves aspects that may seem less positive.

Read 1 Peter 2:11-12 and reread 1 John 3:1, 12-13; 4:1-6

- Can you explain why being God's children might put us in opposition to the world around us, based on 1 John 3:1, 12-13?
- What light does 1 Peter 2:11-12 shed on how we should respond to this situation?
- How does 1 John 4:1-6 help us when we face opposition from the world?

Apply

12. "And now, dear children, continue in him, so that when he appears we may be confident and unashamed before him at his coming" (2:28). How have the passages in this session shown us what it means to "continue in" Jesus?

- How will you press on in continuing in Jesus this week?

Pray

Give thanks to God for the gift of the Holy Spirit in all of us who believe in him, helping us to live in righteousness and in love. Pray that you would be aware and alert to those voices that try to pull us away from God and into sin.

Ask that you would remember to come to him boldly in prayer, confident in his knowledge of you and your status as a child of his. Pray that you would take opportunities to put Jesus' love into action and to help those in need.

5

Perfect Love, Real Faith

1 John 4:7 - 5:5

The Story So Far...

John opened his first letter joyfully, affirming that Jesus is real and we can know the truth about him—and therefore have fellowship with God despite our sin.

He explored three "tests" by which we can have assurance that our faith is genuine—obedience, love, and belief in Jesus—and urged us to remain in Christ.

He challenged us again to obey, love, and believe. Since we are God's children, we should live like it—and we have everything we need in order to do so!

Talkabout

1. How do people tend to define love in our world today? What is good about those definitions? What misses the mark?

Investigate

Read 1 John 4:7-21

2. There are lots of statements about love in this passage. What jumps out
   at you and why?

3. What do we learn about how our love links to God's love?
   * v 7-8

   * v 11, 19

   * v 12, 16b

4. What do we learn about how our love for God links to our love for
   others (v 20-21)?

5. What *is* love, according to verses 9-10?

- What words would you use to describe this love and the impact it has? (Look particularly at verses 9-10 and 17-18.)

Explore More | OPTIONAL

"God is love." But this is not the Bible's only statement that begins "God is…"

📖 **Read 1 John 1:5; Hebrews 12:29**

- How do these statements help us avoid misconceptions about what "God is love" means?

Apply

6. If we live in love, we are like Jesus (v 17). We're *not* Jesus—we can't be an atoning sacrifice for sins—so what does it look like for us to show Jesus-like love?

Getting Personal | OPTIONAL

Take a moment to reflect on Jesus' love and consider its impact on you. What moments in your life or stories in Scripture have most thrilled you with Jesus' love? Ask the Spirit to show you Jesus' love for you as you pray.

Investigate

📖 **Read 1 John 5:1-5 and reread 4:13-16**

7. How do we get to be born of God and to have God living in us (4:13-15; 5:1)?

8. Why does our love for others prove that our faith is genuine?

Getting Personal | OPTIONAL

John's words in 5:1 are challenging! We can convince ourselves that we can have a vibrant relationship with God while remaining indifferent to his people. But John is saying that being a spiritual child of God means being a spiritual sibling to other believers.

What's your attitude to your fellow believers? Who, if you're honest, do you find it hard to love? Take a moment to pray for those people and ask God to grow love for them in your heart.

9. Why is it sometimes hard to be sure that we are really doing the loving thing? Can you think of particular examples?

- How does John say we can know that we are truly acting in love (v 2)? How could that principle help you in the situations you discussed?

God's commands are good—we can trust them. So John says they are not burdensome (v 3). Even so, sometimes it does feel difficult to serve Jesus in the world we live in.

10. What should we do in order to "overcome the world" (v 5)?

Apply

11. How does this passage challenge the following views on love?
   * Love is primarily about feelings.

   * The highest form of love is romantic love.

   * I am loving someone when I affirm them.

12. Why is it exciting to live with love, based on all that you've discussed?

- What will you do this week as a result?

Pray

Praise God for the amazing love of Christ. Without Jesus, we would have no idea what it truly means to love, and we would have no capacity to actually put love into practice. His love comes first!

Use your responses to question 12 to ask for the Spirit's empowerment and guidance as you seek to live with Jesus-like love.

6

Childlike Confidence

1 John 5:6-21

The Story So Far...

Jesus is real, and we can know the truth about him—and therefore have fellowship with God and eternal life despite our sin.

John has explored three "tests" by which we can have assurance that our faith is genuine—obedience, love, and belief in Jesus—and urged us to remain in Christ.

He spent time focusing on what it means to love and exploring how the love we show to others is empowered by the love that God has shown to us.

Talkabout

1. How trusting do you think you are? Do you tend to believe what people tell you or are you more wary?

Investigate

📖 **Read 1 John 5:6-12**

2. John wants us to know that our faith has a rational basis—so he talks about three witnesses. What are they (v 7-8)?

- What do they testify to (v 11-12)?

What does it mean that Jesus came "by water and blood" (v 6)? The most likely explanation of this verse is that the water is a reference to Jesus' baptism and the blood is a reference to his death.

Explore More | OPTIONAL

📖 **Read Matthew 3:13-17 and Mark 15:33-39**

Take a look at these accounts of Jesus' baptism and death.

- What is being communicated here about who Jesus is and why he came?
- What might you have thought about Jesus if you'd been present?

3. In what sense do you think those moments "testify" to what John says in verses 11-12? How would you tell someone what you believe about Jesus and why, based on those two moments?

John's third witness is God's Spirit. The Spirit is a witness in the sense that he led the apostles to record the events of Jesus' life for us in the New Testament. He is also a witness in the sense that he opens our eyes to these truths when we read them.

4. In verse 9, what is John's argument for accepting the testimony of the Spirit?

Getting Personal | OPTIONAL

What has most convinced you personally that Jesus really is who he said he was? How does that connect with what John is saying here?

Apply

5. What can we do to share these three "witnesses" with those who are not Christians? Share your experiences and pool ideas about how to help people to engage with who Jesus really is and the life he offers.

Investigate

📖 **Read 1 John 5:13-21**

6. What does John want us to be confident about (v 13)?

7. What impact will this confidence have on us…
   • as we come before God in prayer (v 14-15)?

   • when we feel afraid of evil (v 18)?

- as we look out at the world around us (v 19-21)?

- when someone among us has sinned (v 16)?

What is the "sin that leads to death"? John is talking about denying Jesus and rejecting his way.

8. How is this different from the sins committed by those who are followers of Jesus?

9. How can we be sure that we really are right to have this confidence that John is talking about (v 20)?

Apply

10. When and why might we be tempted to turn away from Jesus and worship other things (v 21—you might find it helpful to look back at 2:16)?

11. How do John's words help us not to do that?!

12. Based on everything you have read in 1 John, what would you say to someone who lacks assurance of their faith—who is worried they aren't a real Christian or that they aren't good enough for God?

Getting Personal | OPTIONAL

What do you personally most want to remember from your study of 1 John?

Pray

"He is the true God and eternal life" (5:20). Spend some time praising Jesus!

You might find it helpful to listen to a hymn or worship song together. Try "Before the Throne of God Above."

7

Walking Together

2 John and 3 John

The Story So Far...

In John's first letter, he explored three "tests" by which we can have assurance that our faith is genuine—obedience, love, and belief in Jesus.

He explored each of these "tests" in several ways, encouraging us to spot the signs of spiritual health in our lives and challenging us to continue in our faith.

Talkabout

1. Who in your church do you really love, admire, and appreciate, and why?

Investigate

📖 Read 2 John

The "lady" and her "children" (v 1) are most likely a church and its members, rather than individuals.

2. Throughout the letter, how do we see John's love for the believers he is writing to?

- Why does he love them so much? Is it just that he gets on well with them?

3. How does reading verses 1-4 affect the way you read the later parts of the letter? Think about how you might interpret those later parts if you didn't have the opening.
   - v 5-6

   - v 7-9

   - v 10-11

Explore More | OPTIONAL

John is not alone in expressing such affection for those he leads.

📖 **Read Philippians 1:7-8; 2 Timothy 1:1-4; Philemon 1:12**

Those of us privileged to be in some form of Christian leadership can learn from these examples. Do those we serve know how much they mean to us? Are we quick to tell them that we love them?

- What gave Paul such love for those he served?
- How could you learn from Paul as you express your own love to those you serve?

4. John wants to encourage his readers—but he also wants them to know that they are vulnerable (v 7-11). In what sense?

5. What can they do to guard themselves?

Getting Personal | OPTIONAL

What do you think your own vulnerabilities might be as a believer? What voices or ideas have the potential to influence you away from Christ? Perhaps it's jealousy of others' lifestyles, or anxiety about whether you're good enough, or a tendency to get swept up in gossip, or something else entirely.

Apply

6. How can false teaching threaten our own unity and love for each other as believers today?

• What can we do to strengthen our unity?

Investigate

📖 **Read 3 John**

DICTIONARY

Pagans (v 7): non-Christians.

7. What kind of relationship does John seem to have with Gaius?

8. Gaius is "progressing spiritually"—he's spiritually healthy. What do verses 1-5 show us about what spiritual healthiness looks like?

9. How does Diotrephes' behavior (v 9-10) directly contrast with that of Gaius (v 5-6)?

10. What motivates Diotrephes' behavior, and how is this different from the motives mentioned in verses 7-8?

11. How can we make sure we imitate Gaius and others like him, and not Diotrephes and others like him (v 11)?

Getting Personal | OPTIONAL

Who in your church is like Gaius or Demetrius? Who can you look up to and learn from, imitating what is good?

Apply

12. John speaks of working together for the truth (v 8). How is that happening in your church already, and what more could be done to encourage this?

Pray

Pray for your church. Mention individuals to God by name, praising God for them and asking him to continue his work in their lives. You might find it helpful to print a list of church members to look at before you start.

Pray for missionaries you know of. Ask God to strengthen them to work for the sake of Jesus' name. Ask God to help you support and encourage them.

1, 2, & 3 John

John

Joyful Certainty

LEADER'S GUIDE

Leader's Guide: Introduction

This Leader's Guide includes guidance for every question. It will provide background information and help you if you get stuck. For each session, you'll also find the following:

The Big Idea: The main point of the session, in brief. This is what you should be aiming to have fixed in people's minds by the end of the session!

Summary: An overview of the passage you're reading together.

Optional Extra: Usually this is an introductory activity that ties in with the main theme of the Bible study and is designed to break the ice at the beginning of a session. Or it may be a "homework project" that people can tackle during the week.

Occasionally the Leader's Guide includes an extra follow-up question, printed in *italics*. This doesn't appear in the main study guide but could be a useful add-on to help your group get to the answer or go deeper.

Here are a few key principles to bear in mind as you prepare to lead:

- Don't just read out the answers from the Leader's Guide. Ideally, you want the group to discover these answers from the Bible for themselves.

- Keep drawing people back to the passage you're studying. People may come up with answers based on their experiences or on teaching they've heard in the past, but the point of this study is to listen to God's word itself—so keep directing your group to look at the text.

- Make sure everyone finishes the session knowing how the passage is relevant for them. We do Bible study so that our lives can be changed by what we hear from God's word. So, **Apply** questions aren't just an add-on—they're a vital part of the session.

Finally, remember that your group is unique! You should feel free to use this Good Book Guide in a way that works for them. If they're a quiet bunch, you might want to spend longer on the **Talkabout** question. If they love to get creative, try using mind-mapping or doodling to kick-start some of your discussions. If your time is limited, you can choose to skip **Explore More** or split the whole session into two. Adapt the material in whatever way you think will help your group get the most out of God's word.

1

The Real Jesus

1 John 1:1 – 2:2

The Big Idea

The truth about Jesus is readily available to all—we can be completely confident in it. This should bring us great joy!

Summary

As he opens his letter, John is at pains for us to know that the truth about Jesus is readily available to all (1:1-4). Jesus came, really and fully, into the world we all know. He was there for all to see, hear, and even touch. In these verses, John also shows us that this Jesus is divine—he is no less than God himself. He describes him as "the Word of life" and "the eternal life," who "was from the beginning." Jesus was a human with a normal human body, but he was also God.

All of this matters because it means we can truly know who God is. Many people believe that God exists, but John is saying that God has appeared. We can know God because Jesus showed up on earth. More than this, we can have fellowship with God because of Jesus. And we also have fellowship with other believers. Together, we can be in a living relationship with Jesus today through receiving with faith the message John is sharing.

From verse 5, John turns his attention to us, his readers. He wants us to come to terms with our own sin—the reason we needed Jesus.

John tells us that God is light (v 5). There are two meanings here. First, God is the one who discloses ultimate truth to us. We would be in the dark about spiritual matters were it not for the revelation we find in God. Second, God is utterly morally pure—there is no sin (or "darkness") in him.

With this as his backdrop, John outlines three false claims we can make about our sin (v 6-10). We claim that our sin doesn't matter—it doesn't impede our fellowship with God. We claim that our sin is not really who we are. And we claim that our acts of wrongdoing aren't really sinful at all. All three claims are deceptive. So, John wants us to come clean about our sin. The good news is that when we do, God will forgive us and purify us.

We are to grow in holiness as Christians, even though we will not be perfect in this life. John writes "so that you will not sin" (2:1)—he wants us to want not to sin! But he also assures us that when we do sin, we have Jesus, the Righteous One. Jesus is the perfect sacrifice for sins (v 1-2). It is through him that we can have the fellowship with God that John spoke of in 1:3.

Optional Extra

Put a variety of objects into an opaque bag. Have members of the group take turns to feel the shape of the objects and guess what they are without looking in the bag. This activity links with the first half of the study, which explores how we know what Jesus is really like.

Guidance for Questions

1. How do people in today's world try to find out about God, or about the meaning of life?

Here are a few ideas to get you started:

- They search on the internet.
- They explore pagan practices or "spiritual" philosophies.
- They listen to religious leaders, whether in real life or online.
- Many people effectively just make up their own version of God!

2. How does John emphasize the fact that he really knows about Jesus? What words does he use?

John has heard, seen, looked at, and touched Jesus. He asserts this in verse 1 and then repeats it in verses 2 and 3. Jesus' coming to earth was physical and real, and John knew him personally.

3. But it's clear that Jesus isn't like every other person you might see and touch. How does John highlight this? Pick out the key phrases.

- "That which was from the beginning" (v 1): Jesus is eternal.
- "The Word of life" and "eternal life" (v 1, 2): Jesus brings life.
- "Which was with the Father" (v 2): Jesus came from God the Father. He was with him from the beginning.

- "His Son, Jesus Christ" (v 3): Jesus is God's Son. If we have fellowship with the Father, we have fellowship with Jesus, and vice versa.

Explore More

○ **Read John 8:48-59. Why was [Jesus' claim to have existed before Abraham] so controversial to his opponents?**

Jesus was claiming to be God! It is an astonishing claim. No wonder they immediately tried to stone him, which was the punishment for blasphemy.

○ **What else did Jesus say that shows us who he is?**

- *In verses 50 and 54 Jesus explains that God is the one who glorifies him. Jesus did not claim to be greater than the Father—but if the Father seeks to glorify Jesus, that means he is very great indeed!*
- *Jesus also said that life comes from him (v 51). Those who follow him will never see death.*

○ **How did Abraham respond to the thought of Jesus' coming?**

With joy (v 56)—the same joy that John felt as he wrote about Jesus in 1 John. God himself was going to come to earth—it's breathtaking!

---

4. In verses 3 and 4, what is the result of Jesus having appeared and John having seen him and talked about him?

- John (along with others who have

seen Jesus) now has fellowship with him and with God the Father (v 3).

- Those who have received John's message about Jesus now have fellowship with John and the other apostles.
- Those who have received John's message therefore have fellowship with Jesus and the Father as well. It doesn't matter that we have not seen and touched Jesus. We can be in a living relationship with Jesus today through receiving with faith the message John is sharing.
- This leads to complete joy (v 4)!

5. **How could this passage reassure someone who…**

- **is worried that they are not a very good Christian because they don't know enough?**
  John's purpose in proclaiming what he had seen and heard from Jesus was so that we can have fellowship with other believers and with God. In other words, receiving John's message with faith is enough. We do need to know about Jesus in order to have fellowship with him, but we don't need to have some "inside track," special spiritual experiences, or fuller knowledge. There are no tiers within Christianity. Of course, it is healthy and important to grow in our knowledge of the Bible and Christian doctrine—but this is not what saves us!

- **feels sad that they missed out on seeing Jesus in the flesh?**
  John is clear that what he has seen,

he has proclaimed. It doesn't matter that we weren't physically with John to hear and see and touch Jesus, because through John's message, we know everything that matters about Jesus. And more than that, we have real fellowship with Jesus—which is more than can be said for many of the people who were there to hear, see, and touch him in the 1st century.

- **is doubtful about whether God exists at all?**
  The big news of Christianity is that God has *appeared*. He showed up on earth at a certain time and in a certain place. We can believe in God because we believe in Jesus. We can find out whether God exists by considering who Jesus is.

6. **John mentions three claims people might make (1:6, 8, 10). Look at the first claim. Given that John has just said that God is light, what do you think it means to walk in the darkness?**

It means that we are claiming sin doesn't matter. Here's the logic:

- "God is light." This means that he is the one who discloses truth to us. Unless we listen to him, we are in the dark about spiritual matters. So walking in darkness means living without looking at our own sin. It means not living out the truth.
- "In him there is no darkness at all." God being light also means that he is utterly morally pure. There is no moral ambiguity or questionableness in him. He is perfect. Walking

in darkness means turning our back on this perfection and seeking to forge our own moral path instead.

- **What might it look like for someone to claim that they have fellowship with God while walking in the darkness?**

Some claim to know God—have experiences of him, be close to him, be a spiritual person—while not walking in God's ways. They may not acknowledge their own sin, or they may acknowledge it but fail to recognize that it affects their relationship with God. They live as if faith and behavior belong to different compartments.

7. **Look at the claims in verses 8 and 10. What might it look like for someone to make one of these claims, and why are they wrong to do so?**

The first (v 8) could be summed up as "It isn't me." Claiming to be without sin means saying that I am not fundamentally a sinner. Sin may be a feature of some things I do, but it's not who I am. This claim feels instinctively right to many people—surely my true self, deep down, is good? We might blame our flaws on things that have happened to us, or downplay our sin by saying that we have simply made mistakes.

But John says that if we believe this, we deceive ourselves. Our sin goes all the way to the core of us! As Jesus said, "It is from within, out of a person's heart, that evil thoughts come" (Mark 7:21). If we are going to fight against our sin, we need to understand this.

The second claim (1 John 1:10) is "I haven't sinned." This is not a denial of our sinful nature but of sinful behavior. A person might recognize that they have the capacity to sin, but believe that they happen not to. Perhaps they deny that a particular sinful act is sinful (e.g. adultery is just "following my heart"), or perhaps they believe that they have such self-discipline that they actually live sinlessly.

Again, this is a deception. We are making God out to be a liar—since God's word says that all of us have sinned and fall short of his glory (Romans 3:23). We also risk minimizing our need for Jesus. We need his righteousness to be given to us! If we claim that we have not sinned, we are acting as if Jesus did not really need to come.

8. **Instead of making these claims, we should acknowledge and confess our sin. Why do you think this can sometimes be so hard to do?**

This is an open question and you should invite group members to share any ideas they have.

Perhaps the main reason it's so hard to confess our sin is that we don't want to acknowledge that we are sinful! We want people to think well of us, and we want God to think well of us. It is painful to allow our sin to be exposed, and very tempting to cover it up or pretend it doesn't exist.

There may also be practical reasons why we don't manage to confess our sin to one another. We don't necessarily have time set aside for this. We might not have close, trusting relationships with other Christians where we feel safe confessing our sins. It is worth thinking through how we can foster a culture in our churches where these relationships and these conversations are the norm.

- **But what is our great hope and motivation (v 7, 9)?**
  Jesus will forgive us and purify us from all sin. Not just some sin—all sin. All it takes is for us to confess!

9. **What is John's hope for his readers (2:1)? How can we square this with what he has just said?**
   John wants to help us stop sinning. He is clear that we do sin and will sin. But he wants us to care deeply about our sin, to reject it, and to seek to live godly lives.

10. **Look at verses 1-2. When we do sin, why is it significant that Jesus is…**
   - **our "advocate"?**
     We have one who can vouch for us. This word is referring to Jesus' heavenly ministry before the Father. He is like a skillful lawyer, making the case for us before God.

   - **"the Righteous One"?**
     Any advocate worth having needs to be appropriately qualified, and in the case of Jesus he is. An advocate mired in his own sin would be of no use to us. But Jesus is utterly

without sin, and is therefore able to help us with ours.

- **"the atoning sacrifice"?**
  Jesus is the *atoning* sacrifice because the result of his death is our full reconciliation with God. Jesus speaks for us now because he died for us then. His death removes both our sin and God's anger (another word for which is *propitiation*).

11. **When we do sin, what should we do next? How does the identity of Jesus help us in this?**
   We should confess our sin to God—and it will likely be helpful to confess it to others as well.

   Our instinct will always be to minimize the seriousness of sin and its extent in our lives. But remembering who Jesus is and what he has done should give us the confidence to walk in the light—we can acknowledge our sin because we know that it has already been dealt with in Christ.

12. **John wrote all of this "to make our joy complete" (1:4). What makes you feel most joyful or excited in this first part of 1 John?**
   Encourage the group to share what is most exciting for them personally. It may be helpful to split the group into pairs or threes for this. It may be helpful to read the whole passage through again before you share with one another.

2

This Is How We Know (I)

1 John 2:3-11, 15-17

The Big Idea

We can be assured in our faith if our lives display obedience and love—including when our obedience and love are imperfect!

Summary

John wants to reassure his readers. He knows that their faith is real, and he wants to provide tangible assurance for them. Like a doctor, he introduces them to some spiritual tests they need to take so that they can have the comfort of being given the all clear.

In this study we see two of the tests. Verses 3-6 give us the first: "We know that we have come to know [God] if we keep his commands" (v 3). If we long to keep God's commands, desiring to be like Jesus—even though our obedience is not perfect—then we know God, and the truth is in us.

John is not saying that our obedience is what saves us. Rather, our obedience is the evidence of the relationship we already have with God. It doesn't unlock it but flows from it. The more we know God, the more we will want to be like him.

The second test has to do with loving God's people (v 7-11). John describes this as an "old command"—we all know that we ought to love (v 7). Love was how Jesus summed up the entire Old Testament law (Mark 12:29-31). But this

command is also new, because it is being seen in a new light—in Jesus (1 John 2:8). The life of Christ shows us the perfect fulfillment of the command to love.

Again, John is not presuming that we must love each other flawlessly. But we do begin to embody Jesus' love in our own lives. John uses the language of light and darkness to help us understand this (v 9-11). We are either in the light or in the darkness; we either walk in love, seeing people as they truly are, or we live in hatred, allowing our perspective to be clouded. The light switch can only come on when we let the love of Christ shine into our hearts, showing us what love really means.

We need to see that we can't turn toward God's ways without at the same time turning away from those that are contrary. John tells us not to love the world (v 15-17). He is talking about the collective human tendency to turn away from God. There will always be much that is good in human society, but underneath it are "the lust of the flesh, the lust of the eyes, and the pride of life" (v 16). In other words, our natural selves crave what is contrary to God and take pride in temporary things. As we let the love of Christ deeper into our lives, it means pulling away from these false loves and putting the full weight of our lives down on Jesus instead.

Optional Extra

Choose two group members and set them the same challenge—for example, building a tower out of blocks or making a cup of coffee. The winner is the one who completes the challenge quickest. But there's a catch: one of them will be blindfolded while the other can see.

This simple game serves as an illustration of verses 9-11. To help make the link, you could ask the group to notice how we behave differently when we can or can't see.

Guidance for Questions

1. **What might make someone doubt that their faith is really real?**
   Perhaps it's a sin that continues to bother them. Or perhaps someone has said that their church is not as spiritually far along as another church. Perhaps they simply feel far from God or worry that he is not answering their prayers.

2. **These verses give us the first way we can be sure that we know God. What is it?**
   Keeping God's commands; living as Jesus did.

3. **Why might these words seem intimidating?**
   We fail to keep God's commands in countless ways, even when we're consciously wanting to do what he says. The idea that we've got to live as Jesus did is very challenging—who could possibly live up to that?!

4. **Can you think of a time when you've been encouraged by seeing a fellow believer seeking to obey God or seeking to battle sin?**
   This question is designed to help you see obedience in the light John intends. When we look at other believers, we don't usually suspect them of not being real Christians simply because they sin—serious though that sin may be. Rather, we are encouraged by the ways in which they *are* seeking to follow God. We can look at ourselves in the same way—remembering that if we are obeying God's word, even imperfectly, it is a sign that we truly are in Christ.

• **Can you think of a time when you've seen someone who claims to follow Jesus but doesn't seem interested in keeping his commands?**
   Again, this question is designed to help you see things the way John sees them. We should recognize that while many of us obey God's word imperfectly, there are also those who aren't obeying it at all—who are fundamentally opposed to it. Such people are found in the church, claiming to be Christians. We need to make sure this is not us!

5. **Why might it be reassuring to know that what John is about to talk about is an "old command" (v 7)?**
   God isn't going to make new demands on us that we never bargained for. Love has always been commanded.

6. But John also says it is a new command, because "its truth is seen in him" (Jesus) and "the true light is already shining" (v 8). What does this mean?

What John is saying is that in the coming of Jesus, we see the command to love in a way no one ever did before. Love has always been commanded, but now our understanding of love is in much sharper focus because Jesus' love is perfect.

- Why is this reassuring to us as we seek to obey?

We are not left on our own to figure out what love is. We can see it in Jesus! We are not stumbling around in the darkness—Jesus has turned on the light and shown us how to love.

Explore More

○ *Read Mark 12:28-31. Who are we to love and how much?*

We are to love God with all our heart, soul, mind, and strength—in other words, with everything we have! And we are to love our neighbor (that is, those around us) as much as we love ourselves.

7. What could it look like for us to love what Jesus loved and live as he lived, even if we don't do this perfectly?

Encourage the group to think of specific examples from Jesus' life. There's

no need to try to be exhaustive—give people space to express what they find most inspiring about Jesus and to think through how they could put this into practice themselves. As a starting point, you could consider…

- Jesus' prayer life—e.g. Mark 1:35-37.
- Jesus' willingness to help others—e.g. Mark 5:21-43.
- Jesus' willingness to associate with sinners—e.g. Mark 2:15-17.
- the way Jesus stood up for what was right—e.g. Mark 11:15-17.

8. How do we behave differently when we can see in comparison to when we're in the dark?

The person in darkness stumbles around, feeling their way and probably bumping into things. The person in the light walks confidently because they can see where they're going!

- What about spiritual light and darkness—how do we tell whether someone is in one or the other, according to verses 9-11?
  - The person in the light loves their brother and sister (i.e. their fellow-believers). The person in the darkness hates their brother or sister.
  - The person in the light can see where they are going—there is "nothing in them to make them stumble" (v 10). They know the difference between right and wrong. Meanwhile, the person in spiritual darkness is "blinded" (v 11). They can't see where they're

going—they can't see what's truly right and wrong or how to love people truly.

9. **The idea that our love proves whether our faith is genuine might be scary to start with—we might not feel we're loving enough. But how does this light/darkness imagery, with its very clear distinctions, help reassure us?**

We are either in the light or the darkness. John doesn't allow for an in-between state. Someone might feel they have a long way to go in loving people the way Jesus did, but they can still say that they are in the light—they have experienced Jesus' love, and they want to be like that. They know where they're going, even if they don't always get there! Hopefully this is what describes most of us.

10. **When John says "the world," what does he mean? Look at what he says in verse 16 to help you understand this.**

John is not talking about the physical creation, which we are meant to enjoy as a gift from God. No, he means the human environment around us: specifically, the collective human tendency to turn away from God.

In verse 16 John is giving us an insight into our common human nature.

- The lust of the flesh: Our natural selves crave what is contrary to God's design. Being a sinner doesn't just mean that I *do* sinful things but that I *desire* sinful things.

- The lust of the eyes: The cravings we experience within are linked to the enticements we see.

- The pride of life: We take pride in what belongs to this temporary world, investing in worldly things more than in God. We prioritize and take pride in things like the size of our salary, our physical attractiveness, or the achievements of our kids.

11. **What do you think it means that "the world and its desires pass away"? What evidence of this do you see in the world around you?**

The lusts of the flesh and the eyes won't always be with us. Beauty fades, wealth is spent, achievements stop feeling so important. We need to remember that the things of this world that we find so alluring—even good things—have no future.

12. **John writes to reassure his readers as well as to challenge them. So, who do you know who shows evidence of true faith, and what is that evidence? How could you encourage those people this week?**

Try to think of those who you've seen seeking to obey God's word or acting with love toward a brother or sister. Perhaps you could simply tell them what you've seen in them and how encouraged you've felt by the evidence of God's work in their lives!

- **What about those you know who may be feeling doubtful or discouraged? How could** you encourage them from this passage?

- Obedience does not have to be perfect to be real. "If anyone obeys his word [even imperfectly], love for God is truly made complete in them" (v 5).
- Jesus has shown us what perfect obedience and love look like. We have his help and example as we seek to live obediently (v 8).
- You are either in the light or the darkness. If someone feels repentant about their sin and is accepting Jesus' forgiveness, it probably means they are in the light. Even though they are not loving perfectly, they are able to see how they should love, and they want to be like Jesus.

- **What would you say to someone who is dismissing or minimizing their own sin, or treating another believer badly?**
This passage should be a scary read for those who are living in hatred or who are actively disobeying God in another way. They need to be warned that all sin is serious. Nothing can just be swept under the carpet. Minimizing our own sin means we are turning away from the light of Christ and choosing to walk in darkness.

3

This Is How We Know (II)
1 John 2:12-14, 18-27

The Big Idea
We don't need any special knowledge in order to remain in Jesus and gain eternal life. We can be assured of our faith if we believe what the New Testament says about Jesus.

Summary
In verses 18-25, John introduces us to the third test: doctrine, or what we believe about Jesus. "Whoever acknowledges the Son has the Father also" (v 23).

Acknowledging the Son means believing that Jesus is fully God and fully man, the eternal Son of the Father and the promised Christ or Savior. Many people are positive about Jesus but do not believe he is who he claimed to be. But to give him any status less than that of God is disrespecting him. This is why John says that to deny Jesus is also to deny the Father. Jesus reveals and perfectly represents the Father (Colossians 1:15; John 14:9), so we can only know

God if we accept the truth about Jesus.

John explains that there are "antichrists" who deny this truth (1 John 2:18-19). The word "antichrist" literally just means someone who is against Christ. It often refers to a specific opponent who is to come, but here John uses it to describe those who have claimed to be Christians yet have abandoned and rejected the truth about Jesus. When John says "they went out from us," he is not talking about leaving a particular church but abandoning the truth (v 22).

This teaching might be unsettling. Who are we to think we're immune from being led astray like these false believers? But John wants to encourage us. He wants us to be alert, but also encouraged. "I do not write to you because you do not know the truth, but because you do know it" (v 21). John explains that his readers have the anointing of the Holy Spirit, who teaches us the truth (v 20, 27). We have everything we need to remain in Jesus. We simply need to continue to follow the truth about him.

Verses 12-14 wonderfully sum up this message of reassurance. John speaks to older believers ("fathers") and younger believers ("young men"). His message to all of them is: Your sins *have* been forgiven; you *do* know the Father. To those who've been believers for longer, John gives a reminder that they know "him who is from the beginning." God has not changed in all the time they've known him—it's a reassuring truth. To those who are newer in the faith, John encourages them to know that they are strong and that they have already overcome the

evil one through the work of Jesus. They don't need to be afraid for the future.

All these assurances can be ours as well if the word of God lives in us. We don't need any special knowledge or experiences to feel sure about our faith. We simply need to know who Jesus really is.

Optional Extra

Challenge your group with a puzzle that you need a secret code to crack. Write down a message using Morse code, and give a copy to every group member. (You can find out more about Morse code using an internet search.) Give half the group the Morse code key, but leave everyone else in the dark—then see who can decipher the message.

The point is to illustrate the idea of needing special knowledge. In our faith, we don't need any special knowledge to gain eternal life. We just need Jesus!

Guidance for Questions

1. **What would you say makes someone a real Christian? How do you know they are really saved?**
   Don't shut down anyone's answers or try to reach a true conclusion at this point. The aim is simply to get people talking. Consider using a large piece of paper and inviting people to write down words that they would associate with Christians, and then asking which of those matters the most. This might help unpick what we functionally see as crucial, even if we wouldn't actually say that this is what we think.

2. How can we be sure that we know God and have eternal life (v 23-25)?
By believing that Jesus is the Christ— the Savior—and that he is God's divine Son.

3. Why does what we believe about Jesus impact whether or not we truly know God?
- We can't know the truth about God without believing in Jesus. Jesus is the perfect "image of the invisible God" (Colossians 1:15), "the exact representation of his being" (Hebrews 1:3). Jesus himself said, "Anyone who has seen me has seen the Father" (John 14:9). If we believe in God without believing in Jesus, we are believing in a different god, not the God of the Bible.
- We can't have access to God without Jesus. He is the only way to the Father (John 14:6). We can't get to God if we are indifferent to Jesus.

4. What does John say about "antichrists" (people who are opposed to Jesus)? How do we know that their faith is not genuine (v 19, 22)?
- The antichrists "went out from us" (v 19). This doesn't mean that they left a specific church community but that they left the church altogether.
- They abandoned the true teaching of the apostles and denied the Father and the Son (v 22). It's in this sense that they have left the church: they have left the truth. They haven't just walked away from the church for a period. They have rejected the whole truth about Jesus.
- John says that such leaving indicates that the antichrists were never truly believers (v 19)—they never "belonged to us."

Explore More

○ **Read Mark 13:32-37. What does Jesus say about his return?**
No one knows when it will happen.

○ **What impact should it have on us to know that it is "the last hour"?**
We are to have a sense of urgency and heightened awareness. We can't delay living for Jesus!

5. Based on this passage, what might you say to someone who says they respect Jesus but just don't believe he is God?
If Jesus is who he claimed to be— fully God and fully man—then to give him any status less than that *is* disrespecting him. It does not make sense to be broadly positive about Jesus. You either believe in him or you don't.

6. John has shown us what makes a true Christian. How might this challenge us about the way we treat other Christians who have different opinions from us?
There are many different opinions within the church about all sorts of topics—from very important ones to very trivial ones. We are likely

to end up in churches where most people agree with us about certain things, such as baptism and the role of women. But this can sometimes mean that we end up being suspicious of people in other churches with other opinions. John's clarity about what beliefs make a true Christian should challenge us if we have fallen into that trap. "Whoever acknowledges the Son has the Father also" (v 23). The distinctions between us may well be important, but they are not of first importance.

- **What about people who seem to be Christians but, according to John's definition, are not—how do you think we should treat them?**
We should be wary of those who claim to believe but do not actually honor Christ as Lord! Perhaps they simply need to be better taught—once the truth is pointed out to them, they will accept it. If that is the case, we should welcome them but make it clear that they need to accept Jesus before they are truly part of the family. But if there are those who promote false teaching, the Bible warns us to beware, in case we end up being led astray (e.g. Romans 16:17-18; Titus 1:9-11).

7. **What keeps us anchored to the truth (v 26-27, and look back at verse 20)?**
The anointing of the Spirit ensures that we know the truth.

   NOTE: The word "anointing" literally refers to when special oil is rubbed into someone's forehead. It was done to kings and priests in the Old Testament as a way of setting them apart for their service. In the New Testament, we receive the "anointing" of the Spirit when we believe in Jesus. God's Spirit comes to dwell in us. Jesus referred to the Holy Spirit as "the Spirit of Truth" (John 14:17; 16:13)—it is only by the Spirit's ministry that we can know and grasp the truth about Jesus.

8. **Why is this reassuring for those who fear that their faith is weak or vulnerable?**
If we have the Spirit, no further anointing is needed. No truth God wants us to know about him is beyond our access. No crucial revelation will come which is not already available to us. So, we don't need to feel that we need something extra in order to be real Christians. And we don't need to fear being led astray by false teaching. Of course, we do need to be aware of those seeking to deceive us, and not be complacent. But we don't need to be anxious. We already have what we need to remain in the truth.

9. **What does John want his readers to know?**
He wants them to know that they are legitimate, real Christians. They can be sure that they have eternal life.

   More specifically...
- their sins have been forgiven in Jesus' name (v 12).
- they know God (v 13, 14).

- they have overcome the evil one (v 13, 14).
- they are strong (v 14)!
- the word of God lives in them (v 14).

10. Why do you think John chose to direct specific encouragements to specific groups? Why did they need to hear these truths?

To those who've been believers for longer, John repeats his message that "you know him who is from the beginning." God's eternity comes to mean more to us the longer we go on in the Christian life, as we see more and more changes in the world around us. It is a comfort to know that God does not change, and our knowledge of him does not need to change either.

For younger believers, John emphasizes the fact that they have "overcome the evil one." In the years ahead, these newer Christians will face many battles and experience lots of ups and downs. But the crucial battle has already been won. As Jesus said, "In this world you will have trouble. But take heart! I have overcome the world" (John 16:33). So John tells younger believers that in Christ, they are strong. They don't need to fear what lies ahead.

11. What do you find most encouraging in these verses?

Encourage the group to share freely about what most encourages them and why.

12. Are you ever tempted to think that your faith needs upgrading in some way—perhaps that you need special knowledge or experiences?

- How will what we've read in this study help to reassure us, and help us to remain steadfast in the faith we have received?

In a world that loves upgrades, it can be tempting to want to experience new things. But the gospel doesn't need updating. What we heard right back at the beginning is exactly what we still need today. If we honor Jesus as God's Son and our Savior, we have a true faith. All we need to do is to remain in that faith—and we have the Holy Spirit to help us do so.

Of course, remaining in Jesus may well mean growing and changing. There is a sense in which we will experience new things. But we should be reassured that these changes and experiences are not in themselves what proves that our faith is genuine. As you discuss these questions, it may be helpful to encourage the group to pull out particular verses and truths from the passage that they want to remember.

4

Continue in Jesus

1 John 2:28 - 4:6

The Big Idea

As children of God, we will have a family likeness—so we must "continue in him," pressing on in seeking to live righteously, with love, and with clarity about who Jesus is.

Summary

In this study, we will see John's three tests again, this time from a new angle. John wants to encourage us with the truth that we are God's beloved children, born of him! As such, we will start to show a family resemblance. So John urges us to "continue in [Jesus]" (2:28).

He begins by writing with excitement about who we are in Christ (2:28 – 3:3). He marvels at the sheer wonder of being God's children (3:1). One day we will appear before Jesus' throne with confidence (2:28), because we will be like him (3:2)! Knowing our future should motivate us to live righteously in the present—doing all we can to be as similar now to what we will be like then.

Verses 4-10 give us more motives to live righteously. John shows us the nature of sin, what Jesus has done to our sin, and why it is therefore out of place in our lives as Christians. Pursuing sin would be an appalling contradiction of all that Christ came to do for us. This is why John says, "No one who lives in him keeps on sinning" (v 6) and "No one who is born of God will continue to sin" (v 9). He is not saying that we will never sin. He is talking about the trajectory of our lives. If we are children of God, we will see sin as unthinkable.

In verses 11-18, we return to the love test. John urges us not to be like the murderer Cain. Hating a brother or sister amounts to the same thing as murdering, since both actions reveal that we have not "passed from death to life" (v 14). We are either in the light or in the darkness. Acting like Cain is a sign that we are in the darkness. By contrast, true love is seen in Jesus' sacrifice for us (v 16)—and in our own small sacrifices for each other too (v 17-18).

This is all deeply challenging. But John wishes to reassure us (v 19-24). We can know that we do belong to the truth, even when our hearts condemn us for a lack of love. God knows everything (v 20)—he sees our sin, and he has still made us his children. We can have confidence before him even though we fail.

4:1-6 explores the doctrine test. John warns us to "test the spirits"—which we can take to mean every message we hear about Jesus, God, or spirituality (v 1). We should look out for crucial truths: Jesus is from God and has come in the flesh. Anyone or anything which denies these truths is not from God (v 2-3).

We need to be watchful, but we don't need to be afraid. If we are God's children, we have already overcome these anti-Jesus voices. We have the Spirit; we can listen to John and his colleagues, the apostles who wrote the New Testament (v 6). Because of this, we can tell truth from lies.

Optional Extra

Ask every group member to bring in a photo of somebody who is genetically related to them (assuming this is possible for everyone). Jumble them up and see if you can guess whose relative is whose! This links to the first question and introduces the idea that God's children will come to resemble Jesus.

Guidance for Questions

1. **What traits do people in your family have in common? Do you take after older family members? Do younger family members take after you?**
   This is a way of introducing the concept of being God's children. In today's study we will see that God's children grow to take after him.

2. **John wants us to have confidence when Jesus returns (2:28). What will give us this confidence about who we are in him (v 29)?**
   We will have done what is right, and this will prove that we have been "born of him." Why? Because Jesus is righteous—so his children will take after him.

3. **3:1-2 is full of excitement—so what is John excited about?**
   • We are children of God. We

are broken, messy, foolish, have-no-excuses sinners—yet we are now called children of God. In fact, we *are* children of God! It is astounding. The love we receive is out of all proportion to what we could ever have imagined.
   • One day we will see Jesus! We will look our Savior in the eye and see how he looks at us.
   • And this means we shall at last become truly like him. Even now, we are slowly becoming like Jesus. But when we see him fully, the process will be completed.

• **What implications do these truths have for how we live now (v 2-3)?**
   • We live with hope. We know that despite all our failings now, we will one day be made perfectly righteous, like Jesus. It gives us a new perspective as we struggle against our sin.
   • We purify ourselves. This means we do all that we can to be as similar *now* to what we will be like *then*, when we see Jesus face to face. We desire holiness. It's a sure sign of the presence of God in our lives!

4. **In verses 4-10, what does John say about...**

• **what sin is like and where it comes from (v 4, 8)?**
   • v 4: The essence of sin is lawlessness. It is not just breaking specific rules laid out in the Bible—it is a rejection of God's law as a whole. It is a rebellion against God.
   • v 8: Sin comes from the devil. So

when we sin, we are siding with the evil one.

- **what Jesus has done to our sin (v 5, 8)?**
Jesus came to take away our sins and destroy the devil's work (v 5, 8). He has removed our sins from us completely—God can no longer look at us and our sins at the same time.

- **Why is sin therefore out of place in our lives as Christians?**
If we sin, we are actively opposing Jesus' whole purpose in coming to earth. Why would we want to bring back into our lives the very sin Christ went to such lengths to remove from us?

5. **Speaking practically, what can we actually do to oppose sin in our lives?**
Here are some possible ideas:
  - Keep looking at Jesus. We become like what we behold! The more we behold Jesus' righteousness, his compassion, and his holiness, the more we will long to be like him, and the more he will transform our hearts.
  - Keep remembering what Jesus has done. Jesus is utterly opposed to sin—he came to destroy it. The more we understand why Jesus came, and the more we come to terms with the fact that he has removed our sin from us, the less palatable sin will seem.
  - Keep watching out for sin. Perhaps we will ask a friend to keep us

accountable, or perhaps we will put it in our calendar to challenge ourselves over this on a regular basis. We should do anything that will prevent us from allowing sin to gain a foothold in our lives!

- **According to this passage, if we are believers, what is empowering us to oppose sin and do what is right?**
We have been born again in Christ (2:29)—we are new creations! We have a new nature that takes after Jesus, just as a child takes after its biological parent. God's seed is in us (3:9). So we now have a different relationship to sin.

6. **According to verses 11-18, what quality will be displayed by those who are in Christ?**
Love!

- **John gives us a bold definition of love in verse 16. How do you think this compares with how people in the world around us understand it?**
This is an opportunity to have an open discussion about how the world around us perceives love. Group members might talk about romance, sex, feelings, or family.

  It would be helpful to highlight the point that our world's view of love is often very me-focused—whereas John's definition focuses on sacrifice. Jesus laid down his life for us, and so we ought to lay down our lives for each other. This is very different from many (although not all) depictions of love in our culture today.

7. How and why did Cain show the opposite of love (v 12)?
He murdered his brother. Cain belonged to the evil one, which means he rebelled against God. He hated his brother's righteousness because it came from God.

• How does John turn this example into a challenge for us (v 14-15)?
John says that we can be far more like Cain than we think. Whenever we entertain feelings of hatred, we are following in Cain's footsteps.

8. What's another way in which we can fail to show real love (v 17-18)?
It is easy to make grand declarations of love or commitment, or to kid ourselves into thinking we genuinely love our brothers and sisters. But John calls us to love "with actions and in truth," not just in what we say (v 18). This includes showing pity to those who need help.

9. Our hearts may be feeling guilty as we read these words—so what does John say to reassure us, and why is it reassuring?
• v 19-20
God knows everything. He sees every single sin. This means that Jesus knew *exactly* what he was taking on when he got involved with us! We may be discovering fresh depths of sin in our hearts, but none of it is a revelation to Jesus. He has no regrets about being our Savior.

• v 21-22
As we seek to please God, we will find our prayers being answered. This is not a quid pro quo arrangement with God—*You obey me and I'll start giving you stuff.* It is simply that the more we genuinely seek God's will in our lives, the more we will naturally be praying according to that same will.

• v 23-24
God's commands are simple: to believe, and to love. We don't have to perform special rituals or keep lots of difficult rules. We simply have to believe in the name of Jesus and love one another. If we can see the evidence of those things in our lives, we can be confident that we are indeed God's children.

10. What are the two crucial beliefs that John identifies (v 2-3)?
• That Jesus has come in the flesh—i.e. that he is human.
• That Jesus is from God—i.e. that he is divine.

• If someone denies these truths, what does this mean?
They are not from God; they are not a Christian.

11. There are many opinions and voices in the world that are opposed to Jesus. That might seem scary. But how does verse 4 reassure us?
We are from God, and he is greater than the world. It is he who helps us overcome the falsehoods arrayed against us.

Explore More

○ **Can you explain why being God's children might put us in opposition to the world around us, based on 1 John 3:1, 12-13?**

- *v 1: The non-Christian world doesn't "know" us—doesn't really get us. People won't understand what has truly happened to us—what it means to be born again and united to Christ. From their perspective, we've "become religious," or started to follow a historical figure, or got into being pious. So we don't truly belong, and we never can. We're foreigners and exiles (1 Peter 2:11). Being known by Jesus means being less known by the world around us.*

- *v 13: Like Cain's brother, Abel, followers of Jesus live with love and righteousness. This provokes a backlash from the world, since the world is essentially in rebellion against God's ways. If we seek the sort of righteousness John is calling us to, we can be sure it will not meet with universal approval!*

○ **What light does 1 Peter 2:11-12 shed on how we should respond to this situation?**

We must live good lives in the world. We won't retreat from the world entirely but will live "among the pagans," doing life alongside non-Christian friends and colleagues. But we will live differently, in a way that may prove attractive to those who don't yet know the Lord, rather than being sucked in by the ways of the world.

○ **How does 1 John 4:1-6 help us when we face opposition from the world?**

- *John advises us to "test the spirits" (v 1)—to be on the lookout for those who oppose God. How do we do that? The best way is to be so familiar with the truth about Jesus that anything even slightly out of step with that truth will be apparent to us.*

- *John also warns us that "whoever is not from God will not listen to us"—so if we find ourselves being opposed or shut out, we don't need to be shocked or surprised.*

- *Finally, John assures us that we have already overcome the world (v 4) because we are in Christ. We don't need to be worried or afraid. We just need to keep trusting in Jesus.*

---

12. **"And now, dear children, continue in him, so that when he appears we may be confident and unashamed before him at his coming" (2:28). How have the passages in this session shown us what it means to "continue in" Jesus?**

Continuing in Jesus means...

- opposing the presence of sin in our lives.

- loving one another—not just in words but in deeds.

- clinging to the truth that Jesus is both human and divine, and that he came to save us from our sins.

- **How will you press on in continuing in Jesus this week?**
Invite group members to share whatever answers they like, but encourage them to link their responses to what you have studied together.

5

Perfect Love, Real Faith

1 John 4:7 - 5:5

The Big Idea

True love comes from God, which means that we can love like him! It's a wonderful and exciting privilege, and a demonstration that our faith is really real.

Summary

In this passage John shows us how to distinguish true love from false love. He begins by saying that love comes from God; it is fundamental to who God is (4:7-8). We will therefore never come to a full or reliable understanding of love without him. On the other hand, if we do love, it is evidence that we live in him and he in us (v 8, 12, 16).

In verses 9-12 and 16-19, John highlights several aspects of true love (that is, God's love). It is costly—shown most perfectly through Jesus' sacrifice (v 9-10). It is initiating—it takes action, and it always comes first, before our own love (v 10-11, 19). And it is transformative—it changes

us, giving us confidence and taking away fear (v 17-18).

John makes a staggering claim in verse 12: the unseeable God is made visible not only through Jesus but also through our own love for each other. When we love, we are showing something of God to the world. John therefore concludes that anyone who loves God must also love their brother and sister (v 20-21). The credibility of our faith stands or falls on the presence or absence of this love among us.

John explores this further in 4:13-16 and 5:1-5. The tests are now intermingling: it is our beliefs that prove that we are God's children (4:15), but it is also our love, because belief cannot exist without love. If we believe that Jesus is the Christ, then we come to love the Father who sent him. If we love the Father, we will love others who belong to him, too—just as we love the children of our beloved friends and family (5:1). We must be deeply committed to loving our Christian brothers and sisters.

In turn, love cannot exist without obedience. How do we know that we are truly showing love? John's answer is that we will love God and keep his commands (v 2). The most loving thing we can do for another person is to obey God!

In case we feel overwhelmed by this, John reassures us that God's commands are not burdensome—they are not too much for us to cope with, since God's ways are good for us. "Everyone born of God overcomes the world," John writes in verse 4. As we keep our eyes fixed on Jesus, we will overcome the pull of our hearts toward sin.

Optional Extra

Type "Love is..." into an image search engine on the internet and choose a selection of images to print and share with the group. This will help you with questions 1 and 11 in particular.

Guidance for Questions

1. **How do people tend to define love in our world today? What is good about those definitions? What misses the mark?**

In your discussion you will likely cover the following ideas:
- Love is primarily about feelings.
- The highest form of love is romantic (or sexual).
- In order to love someone, I must affirm them.

2. **There are lots of statements about love in this passage. What jumps out at you and why?**

This is an open invitation for each group member to share personally.

3. **What do we learn about how our love links to God's love?**

- **v 7-8**

Love comes from God. In fact, it is fundamental to who he is. It's not just something he does; it's who he is. This means that we can only truly love when we know God's love. It also means that when we do know God, our knowledge of him will teach us how to love.

- **v 11, 19**

God's love came first. His love triggers ours, not the other way around. So God does not love us because we love. He loves us because *he* loves; our love is only ever in response.

- **v 12, 16b**

Our love unites us with God. When we love, we don't just know God—we find that God lives in us, and we in him. We don't just know his love from a distance; we become united with him. This means that, amazingly, God reveals himself to others through us! No one has ever seen God, but when we love each other, we show people what he is really like.

4. **What do we learn about how our love for God links to our love for others (v 20-21)?**

Our love for others is the way we put our love for God into practice.

5. **What *is* love, according to verses 9-10?**

The greatest ever expression of love was when God sent Jesus to die for our sins.

- **What words would you use to describe this love and the impact it has? (Look particularly at verses 9-10 and 17-18.)**
  - It is active, not just a feeling.
  - It is costly—God gave up his only Son.
  - It takes the initiative—God loved us before we loved him (v 10).
  - It is transformative—it brings us life (v 9), atones for our sins (v 10), and removes our fear of judgment (v 17-18). When we trust in Christ, we know that our sin and its consequences have been fully dealt with.

Explore More

- *Read 1 John 1:5; Hebrews 12:29. How do these statements help us avoid misconceptions about what "God is love" means?*
  - *1 John 1:5—God is light, and in him is no darkness at all. So we cannot say that "God is love" means that God is unendingly tolerant. God is sinless and hates sin.*
  - *Hebrews 12:29—God is a consuming fire. So we cannot say that "God is love" means that God should not be feared or that God will not judge wickedness.*

6. **If we live in love, we are like Jesus (v 17). We're *not* Jesus—we can't be an atoning sacrifice for sins—so what does it look like for us to show Jesus-like love?**

Use your answers to question 5 as a springboard for your discussions here. For example:

- Jesus-like love is active, not just a feeling—so how can we make sure we are acting in loving ways, not just *feeling* love or affection toward others?
- Jesus-like love is costly—we should expect to make sacrifices for others, even if they're only small ones.
- Jesus-like love takes the initiative—we are called to love our enemies and those we find difficult, not wait for someone to show love to us before we show love to them.

7. **How do we get to be born of God and to have God living in us (4:13-15; 5:1)?**

By believing that Jesus is the Son of God and that he is the Christ, i.e. the long-promised Savior of the world.

8. **Why does our love for others prove that our faith is genuine?**

If we believe that Jesus is the Christ, we come to love the Father. Our eyes are opened to his kindness and mercy—we can't help loving him! But there is another step in this logic: if we love the Father, we will love others who belong to him, too (v 1). It would be very strange if, when a close friend had a child, you hated that child. We love our friends' children as an extension of our love for our friends. It's the same with our love for God's children—our fellow believers.

9. Why is it sometimes hard to be sure that we are really doing the loving thing? Can you think of particular examples?

Often, we cannot be sure what the result of our actions will be. This makes it hard to know whether what we are doing is really in love. We can particularly hesitate when we know our actions may cause hurt or upset in the short term—for example, disciplining a child or giving some hard-to-hear advice to a friend.

• **How does John say we can know that we are truly acting in love (v 2)? How could that principle help you in the situations you discussed?**

We are truly loving others when we love God and keep his commands. This means that our priority should be to obey God. When we do so, we will automatically be living with love toward our brothers and sisters. So if we are genuinely seeking to obey God, we can rest in the knowledge that we have done our best to love those around us, even if they don't respond well.

It also means that anything that goes against God's commands—however good it feels—is not really love at all. For example, it is not obedient, and therefore it is not loving, to hide the truth from someone just because we know it would upset them. It is not obedient, and therefore it is not loving, to become romantically involved with someone who doesn't share our faith in Christ, or who is of the same sex as us.

10. What should we do in order to "overcome the world" (v 5)?

Simply keep believing in Jesus! True faith in him is the key to overcoming all that is lined up against us—because it's not our resolve we're trusting but his. As we keep our eyes on him, we will overcome.

11. How does this passage challenge the following views on love?

• **Love is primarily about feelings.**

Feelings are not irrelevant to love. But this passage shows us that love *acts*. The Father did not just feel warmly toward us but acted to send his Son into the world (4:9-10). We, too, are called to actively love.

• **The highest form of love is romantic love.**

This passage makes big statements about what love is and how it is expressed. But there is no mention of romantic love here! John talks about two forms of love—God's love for us in sending Jesus, and our love for him and for those around us, particularly our Christian brothers and sisters. The Bible celebrates one-another love in the church far more than it does romantic love.

- **I am loving someone when I affirm them.**

  We can only love when we are obedient to Christ (5:2). That includes loving what he has commanded. So if we affirm something that is sinful, we are not acting with love.

12. **Why is it exciting to live with love, based on all that you've discussed?**

    Because it is an expression of real faith! The more we love, the more we are living in line with God's character and will. We're becoming like Jesus and representing our Father to the world around us. And we're growing in confidence that, since God is working in us in this way, we really are his beloved children.

- **What will you do this week as a result?**

  Encourage the group to really consider how they will put what they have read into practice.

6

Childlike Confidence

1 John 5:6-21

The Big Idea

We can have total confidence that in Christ we have eternal life! And this affects our prayer life, the way we deal with sin, and the attitude with which we engage with the world around us.

Summary

John wants us to be sure that we really do have eternal life if we believe in Jesus. First of all he reminds us that our faith has a rational basis (5:6-10). He speaks of three witnesses to the truth about Jesus. First come water and blood, which probably refer to Jesus' baptism and death—two events where Jesus' identity was declared and his mission made clear (see Matthew 3:13-17; Mark 15:33-39). These events took place in public and before multiple eyewitnesses; God has made the truth of Christ publicly available.

The third witness is the Spirit. The Spirit is the one who led eyewitnesses and apostles to explain the events of Jesus' life for us in the New Testament. The Spirit also opens our own eyes to be able to see and accept these truths. We need this third witness!

Behind all this is the testimony of God himself (1 John 5:9). John points out that "we accept human testimony"—we believe things that people tell us all the time. How much more should we believe what God tells us?

In verses 11-12 John reminds us of the truth that these witnesses point to: "God has given us eternal life, and this life is in his Son. Whoever has the Son has life."

In the final section, John sets out the confidence we can have as those who do believe. First, we have confidence in prayer (v 14-17). We have access to God because Jesus has opened up the way for us to pray. Our prayers will always be heard and answered (v 14-15). There is a caveat here—John talks about asking for "anything," but "according to [God's] will." God does not just pander to our whims. The more we walk with him, the more we will love what he loves, and the more he will give us what we ask.

John particularly encourages us to pray for those who are falling into sin (v 16-17). He makes a distinction between sin that "leads to death" and sin that does not. Sin that leads to death means denying the truth about Jesus and refusing to walk in his ways. Our prayers are better directed to the needs of those who do desire to follow Jesus but still stumble and fall.

In verses 18-21 John speaks about our spiritual security, assuring us of the protection Christ gives us. The evil one cannot harm us. If we have the Son of God, we have eternal life. What could ever compare to Jesus?

Optional Extra

Play the game "Two Truths and a Lie." Each person must present two true facts and one lie about themselves, and everyone else must guess which is the lie. It's a lighthearted way of introducing the theme of when and why we have confidence in what we are being told.

Guidance for Questions

1. **How trusting do you think you are? Do you tend to believe what people tell you or are you more wary?**
This question is simply designed to get people talking. It links to the theme of this study: we can have total confidence that our faith is true.

2. **John wants us to know that our faith has a rational basis—so he talks about three witnesses. What are they (v 7-8)?**
The Spirit, the water, and the blood.

• **What do they testify to (v 11-12)?**
That we have eternal life in Jesus Christ, the Son of God.

Explore More

○ *Read Matthew 3:13-17 and Mark 15:33-39. What is being communicated here about who Jesus is and why he came?*
You will find thoughts on this question within the answers to question 3.

○ *What might you have thought about Jesus if you'd been present?*
This is an open question—no answer is right or wrong!

3. **In what sense do you think those moments "testify" to what John says in verses 11-12? How would**

you tell someone what you believe about Jesus and why, based on those two moments?

- Jesus' baptism and death showed us who he is. At Jesus' baptism, the Father declared from heaven, "This is my Son, whom I love; with him I am well pleased" (Matthew 3:17). So the event of Jesus' baptism bore witness to who he is. Similarly, the death of Jesus bore witness to who Jesus is. The Roman centurion presiding over the crucifixion exclaimed, "Surely this man was the Son of God" (Mark 15:39). In his account Mark pointed out how it was seeing how Jesus died that prompted this confession.

- These two events also show us why Jesus came and what he achieved. His baptism communicated the need for us to be cleansed of our sins, and the fact that Jesus took our place—since he was baptized despite having no sins to repent of. The cross, of course, was the moment when Jesus actually took our sins upon himself. The darkness of the sky signified the importance of what was happening. The tearing of the curtain in the temple showed that access to God was now possible.

- In what sense are these moments "testifying" to Jesus? Both were historical. Neither happened in an obscure corner of the world or behind closed doors, but in public and before multiple eyewitnesses. God has made the truth of Christ publicly available through these two moments in his life.

4. **In verse 9, what is John's argument for accepting the testimony of the Spirit?**

We readily accept the testimony of other people all the time. We ask strangers for directions, follow instructions on food packaging, and believe our friends when they tell us about their week. We constantly take people at their word. That being so, we have even more reason to believe what God tells us about Jesus. No one is more reliable and no message more significant.

5. **What can we do to share these three "witnesses" with those who are not Christians? Share your experiences and pool ideas about how to help people to engage with who Jesus really is and the life he offers.**

Unbelievers need to come into contact with these three witnesses: they need to know who Jesus is and why he came, and they need the Spirit to work in their hearts to open their eyes to the truth.

You could discuss a range of practical ideas for exposing people to these three witnesses. For me, the most direct way is to invite them to go through one of the four Gospels in the New Testament. They will read Spirit-inspired words and find out about the ministry of Jesus from his baptism through to his death and resurrection.

6. **What does John want us to be confident about (v 13)?**

He wants us to know that if we believe in the Son of God, we have eternal life.

7. **What impact will this confidence have on us…**

- **as we come before God in prayer (v 14-15)?**

We will be confident not only in our eternal relationship with God but also in our present one. Because of Jesus, we can approach God as our Father, being certain that he will hear us and answer.

NOTE: There is a caveat here. John talks about asking for "anything," but "according to his will." God is not just a cosmic version of room service, pandering to our every self-indulgent whim. Prayer is not about bending God's will to ours but bending ours to his. As we get to know Jesus, our desires start to become like his; our priorities reflect his. And so we find more and more traction in our prayer life.

- **when we feel afraid of evil (v 18)?**

Because we have Jesus, we can have confidence that the evil one can do us no ultimate harm. That does not mean we won't go through times of temptation or doubt. It is no guarantee against pain and grief in this life. But ultimately we are safe in Christ. The boat may suffer through fierce storms, but Christ will bring it into the harbor.

- **as we look out at the world around us (v 19-21)?**

If this world feels like it is not your true home, you are right! But one day it will be. We can be confident that all will eventually be brought under the rule of Christ (Ephesians 1:10), when earth will at last perfectly reflect heaven above.

- **when someone among us has sinned (v 16)?**

If we are confident that we have forgiveness and eternal life in Christ, we will also have confidence to pray for those who have sinned. We don't need to be afraid of God; he is our kind Father. If we ask him to help us in our struggles, he will.

8. **How is this different from the sins committed by those who are followers of Jesus?**

Denying and rejecting Jesus leads to death because it constitutes a turning away from the very means by which we can receive life. You are either accepting God or rejecting him; and if you are walking away, you are walking toward death.

9. **How can we be sure that we really are right to have this confidence that John is talking about (v 20)?**

Because we know him who is true. Do you love Jesus? Do you seek to walk in his ways? Then you can be confident that you have eternal life and a relationship with the true God. Nothing more is needed; the Son of God himself gives us understanding.

10. **When and why might we be tempted to turn away from Jesus and worship other things (v 21— you might find it helpful to look back at 2:16)?**

There are all sorts of things in this world that may tempt us to turn away from Jesus. In 2:16 John mentioned "the lust of the flesh, the lust of the eyes, and the pride of life." We can be distracted by the things we want— whether it's a good thing, like a nice house or success in a work project, or a sinful thing, like a sexual relationship outside of marriage. We start to focus on these things more than we focus on the Lord. Or we make deliberate choices to choose our own way instead of God's.

11. **How do John's words help us not to do that?!**

John reminds us that Jesus is "the true God and eternal life" (5:20).

What else could ever compare to him? Or, as the apostle Peter once said, "To whom [else] shall we go?" (John 6:68).

12. **Based on everything you have read in 1 John, what would you say to someone who lacks assurance of their faith—who is worried they aren't a real Christian or that they aren't good enough for God?**

Of course, the answer to this question will depend on what their life is like. Remember John's three tests: obedience, love, and belief in Jesus as God's Son. If a person shows signs of these three things, then they can be assured of their salvation, even though they still go wrong in lots of ways.

Walking Together

2 John and 3 John

The Big Idea

Walking in the truth means walking in unity and love with other believers. This will happen as we guard against false teaching and as we welcome one another for the sake of Jesus.

Summary

John's second and third letters are addressed to more specific groups of people and therefore give some more specific, practical pointers.

The "lady" and her "children" to whom John addresses his second letter are most likely a church and its members (2 John 1:1). It is clear that John deeply and sincerely loves these believers. Although he will give them commands, he does not speak like an employer or instructor but a dear friend. This love comes from the unity they have in Christ: John loves them "in the truth" and "because of the truth" (v 1-2).

After encouraging them about their own faithfulness to that truth (v 4) and spurring them on to continue in it (v 5-6), John moves to the main topic of his letter: these believers are vulnerable (v 7-11). There are false teachers who do not acknowledge Jesus Christ and who pose a spiritual threat to the church. John reminds the believers to continue in the truth and watch out for anyone who has abandoned it (v 7-9). He instructs them to keep a healthy distance from these teachers and not to welcome them into their church (v 10-11).

John concludes his letter with a final expression of affection—his desire to see these readers soon (v 12).

3 John is in some ways the flipside of 2 John. It is written to an individual rather than a church; and while 2 John discouraged hospitality to false teachers, 3 John commands hospitality for faithful teachers.

John begins by commending Gaius, the letter's recipient (1:1-5). He has heard about Gaius' spiritual health. It seems that Gaius' faithfulness to the truth is particularly shown by his love and hospitality. John zeroes in on this in verses 6-8. Gaius has been showing hospitality to Christian visitors; they are presumably missionaries since they have gone out "for the sake of the Name" (v 7). Through his love and welcome, Gaius has been working together with these missionaries, becoming part of God's mission himself (v 8). John contrasts this with the behavior of Diotrephes (v 9-10), who refuses to welcome missionaries.

John encourages Gaius to imitate what is good and not what is evil, mentioning Demetrius as an example of what is good (v 11-12). As with his previous letter, he closes with an expression of affection and a desire to see Gaius soon (v 13-14).

Optional Extra

Print out a list of church members ready for the prayer time.

Guidance for Questions

1. **Who in your church do you really love, admire, and appreciate, and why?**

   John's second and third letters explore what it means to walk in the truth together as a church community—so this question is a way of helping you to think about your own church community and to start to see how people in your church are already living the kind of life that John commends.

2. **Throughout the letter, how do we see John's love for the believers he is writing to?**

   - v 1: He calls them those "whom I love."
   - v 4: He feels great joy when he hears about their faith.
   - v 5: He addresses them as "dear lady."
   - v 12: He longs to visit them and see them face to face.

   - **Why does he love them so much? Is it just that he gets on well with them?**

     He loves them "because of the truth, which lives in us and will be with us for ever" (v 2). This truth is more than simply that which is factually correct. He is speaking about the truth of the gospel, and he is speaking about Jesus, the embodiment of truth. Jesus and the truth about him dwell in John and his readers in such a way that they are bound together fundamentally and irreversibly. Only the truth of Jesus can create such profound love!

     John's affection is also boosted by the joy he feels at knowing that they are faithfully walking in the truth (v 4).

3. **How does reading verses 1-4 affect the way you read the later parts of the letter? Think about how you might interpret those later parts if you didn't have the opening.**

   - **v 5-6**

     When we see the word "command" repeated in these verses, it might make us think of a sergeant major, a dictatorial ruler, or a strict schoolteacher. But verses 1-3 make it clear that although John is writing commands to these believers, he is not simply their boss or instructor. His relationship with them is one of affection, not simply of position and function. So, we can be sure that these commands are affectionately given and motivated by love. We don't need to worry about accepting them.

   - **v 7-9**

     Without verses 1-4, we might worry that John is writing disapprovingly, to tell us off. But when we remember that he writes of his readers' faithfulness to the truth (v 4), we can be sure that his motivation is to spur us on in what we are (hopefully) already doing!

- **v 10-11**

  John's instructions to exclude certain teachers from the church's gatherings might seem harsh at first. But when we realize that he is writing out of love, and that his love stems from the truth he and his readers share, we can see why he speaks so strongly about false teachers. He loves that his readers are walking in the truth, and he can't bear the thought that their unity in the gospel could be disrupted.

Explore More

- *Read Philippians 1:7-8; 2 Timothy 1:1-4; Philemon 1:12. What gave Paul such love for those he served?*
  Just like John, Paul's love for other believers is energized by his love for God.

- *How could you learn from Paul as you express your own love to those you serve?*
  One thing we learn from Paul is to pray for those we serve—and then tell them we are praying for them and giving thanks for them. Another is to remind them of the gospel, as Paul does in Philippians 1:7 and 2 Timothy 1:1-2.

4. **John wants to encourage his readers—but he also wants them to know that they are vulnerable (v 7-11). In what sense?**
   They are vulnerable to false teachers who "do not acknowledge Jesus Christ as coming in the flesh" (v 7).

5. **What can they do to guard themselves?**
   - They need to "watch out" (v 8), making sure they are not led astray.
   - They are to keep a healthy distance from the false teachers (v 10-11).
   - NOTE: We need to remember that John is writing to a church. At first glance verses 10-11 might seem to be about not welcoming unbelievers into our homes. But in reality, this is about not welcoming *deceivers* into our *churches*. Such people are not to be given any form of influence in our fellowship.

6. **How can false teaching threaten our own unity and love for each other as believers today?**
   In our secular culture, we are surrounded by influences that "do not acknowledge Jesus Christ as coming in the flesh" (v 7). When we allow ourselves to be influenced by those outside voices, it can disrupt our unity as believers. For example, someone might become jealous of the lifestyle of non-Christians, causing them to pull back from committing to their church so that they can have more time and money for themselves. Someone might get swept up in political messaging, causing them to downgrade Christ's priorities and mission in favor of more earthly concerns.

   There are also voices from within the church that can lead us astray and cause disunity. For example, some claim that we need special experiences or insider knowledge to be "real Christians." If you believe that, you will either feel inadequate and think you are not really part of the family of believers, or you will feel proud and begin to look down on other Christians. Both responses lead to disunity.

- **What can we do to strengthen our unity?**
  John urges us to be careful and watchful (v 8) and to continue in the true teaching of Christ, which we read in the New Testament (v 9). This might mean studying the Bible more formally or more often together, for example. It might mean being more intentional about praying for one another (or praying for the leaders of the church) that we will remain steadfast in the truth.

  Make sure that your group notices the fact that John also commands us simply to love one another (v 5). We can put one another first, looking out for ways in which we can encourage, support, and help the other believers in our church community.

7. **What kind of relationship does John seem to have with Gaius?**
   He is well known and much loved by John—they are dear friends (v 1, 5), and it is obvious how much affection John has for him. John calls him one of "my children" (v 4), so presumably John has a fatherly role in Gaius' life in some way.

8. **Gaius is "progressing spiritually"— he's spiritually healthy. What do verses 1-5 show us about what spiritual healthiness looks like?**
   Gaius is characterized by faithfulness. He is faithful to the truth (v 4) and faithful to other believers (v 5).

9. **How does Diotrephes' behavior (v 9-10) directly contrast with that of Gaius (v 5-6)?**
   The most obvious contrast has to do with hospitality. Gaius has been exemplary in his hospitality to Christian visitors, even though he didn't know them. They were most likely missionaries who were passing through (since they went out "for the sake of the Name", v 7). We can imagine that Gaius housed and fed these visitors, which would not have been an insignificant expense. Diotrephes, by contrast, refuses to welcome other believers and even tries to get rid of those who are more hospitable (v 10). He wants the focus to be on himself—the opposite of true hospitality, where the needs of others are put before one's own.

10. **What motivates Diotrephes' behavior, and how is this different from the motives mentioned in verses 7-8?**
    Verse 7 talks about missionaries who have gone out "for the sake of the Name" of Jesus. They are motivated by the reputation of Christ, who deserves to be known.

    In verse 8, John says that the motive for showing hospitality to missionaries is "so that we may work together for the truth." John, Gaius, and others like them are becoming part of the work of these missionaries, simply by welcoming them and supporting them.

By contrast, Diotrephes loves to be first. He is more interested in himself than he is in Jesus or in the mission of the church.

11. **How can we make sure we imitate Gaius and others like him, and not Diotrephes and others like him (v 11)?**

We need to resist a Diotrephes-like "me first" spirit and be ready to deny ourselves in service of Christ. How do we do this? By imitating what is good. We can intentionally look up to and learn from believers like Gaius and Demetrius (v 12).

12. **John speaks of working together for the truth (v 8). How is that happening in your church already, and what more could be done to encourage this?**

You might discuss…

• supporting missionaries.

• showing hospitality to one another.

• living in a way that honors Jesus as Lord—with love and goodness.

• speaking about Jesus to unbelievers around us.

• speaking about Jesus to one another!

Go Deeper with the Expository Guide to
1, 2, & 3 John
by Sam Allberry

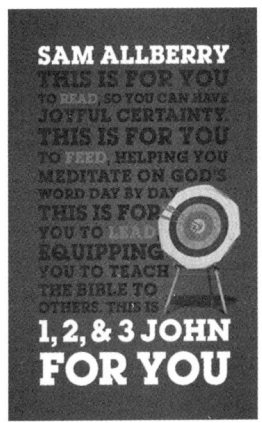

Less academic than a traditional commentary, this expository guide by Sam Allberry takes you verse by verse through the letters of John, helping you to gain joyful certainty that you are God's beloved child.

This flexible resource can enrich your personal devotions, help you lead small-group studies, or aid your sermon preparations.

Explore the God's Word For You series

thegoodbook.com/for-you
thegoodbook.co.uk/for-you
thegoodbook.com.au/for-you

Explore the Whole Range

Old Testament, including:

New Testament, including:

Topical, including:

   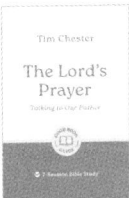

Flexible and easy to use, with over 50 titles available,
Good Book Guides are perfect for both groups and individuals.

thegoodbook.com/gbgs
thegoodbook.co.uk/gbgs
thegoodbook.com.au/gbgs

COMPANY

BIBLICAL | RELEVANT | ACCESSIBLE

At The Good Book Company we are dedicated to helping Christians and local churches grow. We believe that God's growth process always starts with hearing clearly what he has said to us through his timeless and flawless word—the Bible.

Ever since we opened our doors in 1991, we have been striving to produce resources that are biblical, relevant, and accessible. By God's grace, we have grown to become an international publisher, encouraging ordinary Christians of every age and stage and every background and denomination to live for Christ day by day and equipping churches to grow in their knowledge of God, their love for one another, and the effectiveness of their outreach.

Call one of our friendly team for a discussion of your needs or visit one of our local websites for more information on the resources and services we provide.

Your friends at The Good Book Company

thegoodbook.com | thegoodbook.co.uk
thegoodbook.com.au | thegoodbook.co.nz